25
Anti-Aging
SMOOTHIES
For Revitalizing, Glowing Skin

Author

Sarah Koszyk, MA, RDN

Dedication

To my youthful husband, Tomas, whose effervescent glow is always shining.

To Leah Walton, who helped make this book possible with her creativity.

To my mom, Carol Koszyk, for her keen eye.

CONTENTS

39 OMEGA-3

47 POLYPHENOLS

54 CONCLUSION

55 BIOGRAPHY

56 ACKNOWLEDGEMENTS

INTRODUCTION:

W hat you eat matters to your health. The food we put into our bodies affects us in many ways from a glowing complexion, to protecting our skin, to hydrating us, and more. Certain foods are "age-defying", meaning they help our skin look better because they improve cell regeneration and help prevent cell damage. These foods have antioxidants which are substances that inhibit oxidation and counteract the deterioration of living organisms. Vitamins E & C also help to prevent and remove potentially damaging oxidizing agents in order to keep our skin fresh and healthy. Nourishing food is a great source to naturally get antioxidants and vitamins into our bodies. There is an additional bonus from eating foods rich in nutrients. It is the joy that it brings to our heart and soul. Since a smoothie is a very "quick" meal to make, you can take a moment to enjoy the aromas of the ingredients as you prepare them. This can add to your happiness, and being happy is also beneficial to your health.

Growing up in Hawaii, I was constantly outside enjoying the sun and surf. While my mom was diligent about using sunscreen on my Caucasian, olive skin, I still got some damage from the sun. Luckily, living in Hawaii, we were also surrounded by many fruits and vegetables that naturally contained the antioxidants and vitamins which protected our skin. We were blessed to eat many of those foods on a daily basis, thus setting up my future-self with an age-defying complexion.

Since my youthful days, I strive for ways to naturally be "wrinkle free" and protect my skin. Food is a great tool for this. We need to eat to survive, so why not fill our bellies with delicious, nutritious foods that also have a dual-purpose to keep us as youthful as possible?

In this book, 25 Anti-Aging Smoothies For Revitalizing, Glowing Skin, you'll find 5 key ingredients, such as Vitamin E, Vitamin C, Beta-Carotene, Omega-3 Fatty Acids, and Polyphenols, which all contribute to healthy, vibrant, radiant skin. Each ingredient has 5 smoothie recipes specifically made to blast your system with that nutrient to get your skin glowing.

Also take note that within each smoothie category, you'll not just get that vitamin or antioxidant, you'll also have many other antioxidants and vitamins present to further enhance and optimize your skin. Each smoothie contains multiple anti-aging properties from Omega-3s to Vitamins C & E and more. By combining the wonderful foods suggested, you'll receive plenty of benefits for long-lasting, vibrant skin.

I'm excited to take you on this "Smoothie Journey" towards health, wellness, and luscious beauty from the inside out. Get ready for fresh, strong, and hydrated skin.

SMOOTHIES

Smoothies are a great way to start the day and get a healthy dose of fruits and vegetables. Smoothies are quick, easy, delicious, and very family-friendly.

D uring spring and summer seasons when fruits and vegetables are abundant, I prefer to use fresh produce. However, in the fall and winter months, frozen fruits and veggies provide a great source of nutrients and add to the chilled, smoothie texture and temperature. Even in the spring and summer, you can still incorporate frozen fruits and vegetables into your smoothie for the chill-factor.

With so many smoothie variations out there, you have a lot of freedom and creativity in order to make a nourishing, satisfying, and tasty smoothie. One of the best parts about smoothies is learning how easy it is to combine both fruits and vegetables into one drink. The result is a delicious meal or snack that is relatively simple to prepare. There are some key components to a well-balanced smoothie. Here they are:

Key Components for a Well-Balanced Smoothie:

#1. Colors: A smoothie should have some type of color from fruits and/or vegetables. The different colors of the rainbow provide you with different antioxidants, vitamins, minerals, and phytochemicals*. Fruits have natural sugars in them and provide sweetness to the drink. In order to keep your sugar intake in balance, the recommended individual serving amount per smoothie is about 1-2 cups of fruit. This will provide 15-45 grams of sugar depending on the fruit choice.

*Phytochemical Definition: A biological compound found in plants that help protect the plant from various elements and can be beneficial to protecting human health, too.

#2. Heart-Healthy Fats: Fat is an essential part of our overall nutrition, and we need some fat to assist with processing our fat-soluble vitamins. For example, Vitamin E, A, D, and K all require fat in order to adequately get metabolized by the body. Therefore, by incorporating a little bit of fat into your smoothie, you will optimize the absorption of the fat-soluble vitamins in the fruits and vegetables. For this reason, all of the smoothies in this book have a source of heart-healthy fat. Fats also provide nourishment and satiety. So the addition of fat will provide you with a complete meal in just one glass.

#3. Fiber: Fiber provides many benefits such as normalizing our bowel movements, helping us control our blood sugar levels, and aiding us to feel full and satisfied. Since fiber fills us up, we may have the need to eat less which can also help with weight management. Fiber can be found in fruits, vegetables, nuts, and seeds. Each one of these smoothies is chock-full of fiber to fabulously benefit your body.

#4. Protein:

Protein is important for nail and hair growth, maintaining our lean muscle mass, and acting as a building block for our muscles and skin. When we combine carbohydrates from fruits and vegetables with protein intake, the protein actually helps with the uptake of the carbohydrates; and the carbohydrates get metabolized faster resulting in optimal nutrition utilization.

*When to drink the smoothies? If incorporating a scoop of protein into every smoothie recipe, each of these smoothies can be used as a meal replacement for breakfast, lunch, or dinner. Or you can just drink the smoothie as a hearty snack with or without the added protein.

I strongly recommend adding a protein powder to all of the following smoothies. By including a protein powder with the smoothies, you can also turn these smoothies into a complete meal. I recommend purchasing protein powders made from non-GMO, organic sources. You can use a Whey-Protein Powder if you are an omnivore or a vegetarian. For vegans, try a 100% Pure Pea Protein or Brown Rice Protein or Hemp Protein Powder. To keep the desired flavor combinations of the smoothies in this book, I recommend buying a non-flavored protein powder. When buying a protein powder, look at the nutritional label for products offering between 15 - 25 grams of protein per serving.

Sample Nutritional Label *(the protein is usually at the end)*

Nutrition Facts	
Serving Size 1 scoop (33g)	
Servings Per Container	
Amount Per Serving	
Calories 120	Calories from Fat 18
	% Daily Value
Total Fat 2g	
Saturated Fat 0g	
Trans Fat 0g	
Cholesterol 0mg	
Sodium 330mg	
Total Carbohydrate 1g	
Dietary Fiber 0g	
Sugars 0g	
Protein 24g	

Now that you know the 4 key components to making a healthy smoothie that can constitute a meal, let's take a look at the 5 anti-aging properties that will keep your skin youthful and glowing.

*All of the smoothies in this book are gluten-free, dairy-free, soy-free, and vegan in order to accommodate most people. Each smoothie is less than 300 calories. I will be adding tips for substitutions if you choose to use another product that contains dairy or soy.

VITAMIN E

Vitamin E helps the skin retain moisture and protects it from the harmful effects of free radicals. Vitamin E is fabulous for protecting the cells from damage and keeping our skin vitalized.

**The recommended daily allowance of Vitamin E is 15 milligrams for both men and women over the age of 14 years old, according to the US Food and Drug Administration.

Sources of Vitamin E include:

Food	Milligrams (mg) Per Serving	Percent Daily Value
Sunflower Seeds, dry roasted, 1 ounce	7.4	49
Almond Milk, 1 cup	7.3	49
Almonds, dry roasted, 1 ounce	6.8	45
Peanut Butter, 2 Tablespoons	2.9	19
Beet Greens, 1 cup	2.6	17
Pumpkin Puree, 1 cup	2.6	17
Red Peppers, raw, 1 cup	2.4	16
Avocado, ¼ of an avocado	2.0	13
Kiwi, 1 medium	1.1	7
Mango, sliced, ½ cup	0.7	5
Spinach, raw, 1 cup	0.6	4

This smoothie is bursting with Vitamin E and guaranteed to help you feel rejuvenated and revitalized.

Ingredients:

1 cup of tightly packed spinach (Vitamin E)
½ medium, ripe banana
2 Tablespoons avocado (peel and pit removed) (Vitamin E)
1 Tablespoon sunflower seeds (Vitamin E)
2 Tablespoons lemon juice
1 cup of unsweetened almond milk (Vitamin E)

Directions:
Put everything in a blender. Blend and pour.

Nutrient Facts:
210 calories
26 grams of carbohydrates
7 grams of fat
5 grams of protein
6 grams of fiber

2 Tropical Pumpkin Smoothie

Coconut and banana lend a tropical twist to the favorite fall squash—pumpkin. The canned variety can be found all year long, so no need to wait for this treat.

Ingredients:

½ cup coconut yogurt or Greek yogurt (dairy option)
½ cup canned pumpkin puree (Vitamin E)
¼ teaspoon ground cinnamon
½ medium, ripe banana
1 Tablespoon ground flaxmeal

Directions:
Put everything in a blender. Blend and pour.

Nutrient Facts:
285 calories
43 grams of carbohydrates
7 grams of fat
16 grams of protein
7 grams of fiber

The mixed berries provide a powerhouse of flavor, while the greens pack a major punch on the Vitamin E front. The combo will leave you glowing from the inside out.

Nutrient Facts:

230 calories
39 grams of carbohydrates
7 grams of fat
7 grams of protein
8 grams of fiber

Ingredients:

1 cup fresh or frozen mixed berries
½ cup tightly packed spinach (Vitamin E)
½ cup beet greens* (Vitamin E)
½ medium, ripe banana
½ cup unsweetened almond milk (Vitamin E)
1 teaspoon olive oil (Vitamin E)

Directions:

Put everything in a blender. Blend and pour.

*This is a great way to use the beet greens from whole beets. You don't need to throw the stems away. They taste great in a smoothie.

Every ingredient in this smoothie contributes to the velvety smooth mouth feel. As a bonus, the avocado and sunflower seeds can help your skin stay velvety smooth, too.

Ingredients:

2 Tablespoons avocado (peel and pit removed) (Vitamin E)
1 Tablespoon sunflower seeds (Vitamin E)
1 medium, ripe banana
½ cup light coconut milk

Directions:
Put everything in a blender. Blend and pour.

Nutrient Facts:
209 calories
30 grams of carbohydrates
10 grams of fat
4 grams of protein
5 grams of fiber

5 Strawberry, Mango, and Red Pepper Smoothie

This smoothie recipe is fresh and exciting. Red pepper and hemp seeds add an unexpected twist to a classic smoothie.

Ingredients:

½ cup mango (frozen or fresh with peel and pit removed) (Vitamin E)
1 cup fresh or frozen strawberries
½ red pepper (seeds removed, roughly chopped) (Vitamin E)
1 cup unsweetened almond milk (Vitamin E)
1 Tablespoon hemp seeds

Directions:
Put everything in a blender. Blend and pour.

Nutrient Facts:
282 calories
41 grams of carbohydrates
10 grams of fat
13 grams of protein
15 grams of fiber

TIP: Get creative with your smoothies. Once you've mastered the basics, you can mix and match ingredients.

For example, instead of using hemp seeds, try chia seeds or ground flaxmeal. Instead of using strawberries, try blueberries, blackberries, raspberries, or a berry medley.

VITAMIN C

Vitamin C improves cell growth. One study even suggested that a diet high in Vitamin C can result in fewer skin wrinkles. Vitamin C also helps regenerate other vitamins in the body, such as Vitamin E. Since Vitamin C is water-soluble, the body does not store it, and any excess will be eliminated in your urine. It is important to eat a continuous supply of Vitamin C every day to protect your skin, heal wounds, and repair damaged bones and teeth. If you do eat foods with Vitamin C throughout the day, you will maximize the benefits of this vitamin for your body.

**The recommended daily allowance of Vitamin C is 60 milligrams for both men and women over the age of 4 years old, according to the US Food and Drug Administration.

Sources of Vitamin C include:

Food	Milligrams (mg) Per Serving	Percent Daily Value (Based off Male)
Strawberries, 1 cup	104	173
Papaya, ½ fruit	94	157
Kiwi, 1 large	84	140
Purple Cabbage, raw, 1 cup	54	90
Grapefruit, ½ fruit	38	63
Blueberries, 1 cup	14	23
Lemon Juice, ¼ cup	12	20
Spinach, 1 cup	8	13
Mint, 2 Tablespoons	1	2

This cheerful recipe is perfect to drink on a hot day. Actually, it is just perfect, period.

Ingredients:

1 cup fresh or frozen blueberries (Vitamin C)
1 cup fresh or frozen strawberries (Vitamin C)
1 cup coconut water or regular water
1 Tablespoon lemon juice (Vitamin C)
1 teaspoon chia seeds
1 handful of mint (leaves only) (Vitamin C)

Directions:
Put everything in a blender. Blend and pour.

Nutrient Facts:
162 calories
36 grams of carbohydrates
3 grams of fat
3 grams of protein
9 grams of fiber

7 Refreshing Papaya-Strawberry Smoothie

This vibrant smoothie is a refreshing pick-me-up for your day and your skin.

Ingredients:

½ cup papaya (Vitamin C)
1 cup fresh or frozen strawberries (Vitamin C)
½ cup coconut yogurt or Greek style yogurt (dairy option)
¼ cup coconut water or regular water
1 Tablespoon hemp seeds

Directions:

Put everything in a blender. Blend and pour.

Nutrient Facts:
203 calories
29 grams of carbohydrates
5 grams of fat
14 grams of protein
9 grams of fiber

8 Tangy Grapefruit and Basil Smoothie

The kiwi, grapefruit, and basil play nicely together in this recipe. The taste of each flavor is identifiable without being overpowering. All of the ingredients come together in a beautiful marriage in your mouth.

Ingredients:

1 cup kiwi (peel removed) (Vitamin C)
½ cup grapefruit (peel and seeds removed) (Vitamin C)
4 leaves of basil
1 cup tightly packed spinach (Vitamin C)
1 Tablespoon chia seeds

Directions:
Put everything in a blender. Blend and pour.

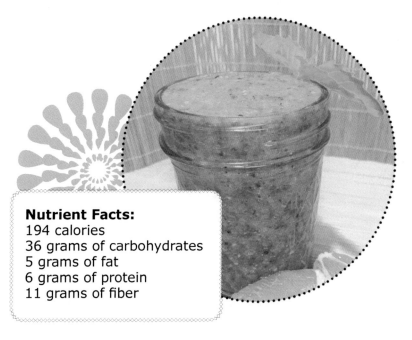

Nutrient Facts:
194 calories
36 grams of carbohydrates
5 grams of fat
6 grams of protein
11 grams of fiber

9 Berry, Spinach, and Almond Smoothie

The blueberries lend antioxidant properties and fresh flavor, while the almonds and spinach add heartiness.

Nutrient Facts:
237 calories
30 grams of carbohydrates
10 grams of fat
13 grams of protein
10 grams of fiber

Ingredients:

1 cup frozen blueberries (Vitamin C)
1 cup tightly packed spinach (Vitamin C)
1 cup unsweetened almond milk
6 almonds

Directions:

Put everything in a blender. Blend and pour.

No need to fall into a citrus and berry rut to get in your Vitamin C. Purple cabbage yields a good amount of Vitamin C and adds a striking color to this smoothie.

Ingredients:

1 small, green apple (cored and cubed)
¾ cup purple cabbage (roughly chopped) (Vitamin C)
½ cup frozen blueberries (Vitamin C)
1 Tablespoon chia seeds
½ cup coconut water or regular water

Directions:
Put everything in a blender. Blend and pour.

Nutrient Facts:
245 calories
45 grams of carbohydrates
5 grams of fat
7 grams of protein
13 grams of fiber

TIP: Here are some ingredients to add to your smoothie to provide additional flavors:

Spices: Cinnamon, Cardamom, Nutmeg, Allspice

Herbs: Basil, Mint, Oregano, Dill, Thyme, Parsley, Cilantro

Vanilla: Vanilla assists with flavor and adds that extra pizazz

BETA-CAROTENE

Beta-Carotene, a carotenoid antioxidant, protects cells from damage and assists with better eyesight. Carotenoids typically give fruits and vegetables vibrant orange and green colors. Once people consume beta-carotene, it gets turned into Vitamin A in the body. Vitamin A is necessary for maintaining skin health and a youthful appearance.

**While beta-carotene does not have a structured recommended daily allowance, Vitamin A does. The recommended daily allowance of Vitamin A is 900 micrograms for men and 700 micrograms for women over the age of 19 years old, according to the US Food and Drug Administration.

Sources of Beta-Carotene include (these values are based off Vitamin A values):

Food	Micro-grams (mcg) Per Serving	Percent Daily Value (Based off Male)
Pumpkin Puree	6,867	763
Kale	1,197	133
Spinach, 1 cup	504	56
Carrot, raw, ½ cup	459	51
Cantaloupe, ½ cup	135	15
Mango, raw, 1 whole	112	12

When you are crunched for time, this no-fuss smoothie is an easy way to pack in beta-carotene rich vegetables.

Ingredients:

1 cup kale (only take the leaf part and leave out the stem) (beta-carotene)
1 carrot (chopped) (beta-carotene)
1 green apple (core removed and chopped)
Lemon juice from 1 lemon or 2 Tablespoons lemon juice
1 cup coconut water or regular water
1 Tablespoon hemp seeds

Directions:
Put everything in a blender. Blend and pour.

Nutrient Facts:
191 calories
34 grams of carbohydrates
5 grams of fat
6 grams of protein
12 grams of fiber

This recipe is inspired by flavors of the Far East. Ginger and the optional turmeric give some spice and interest to this smoothie while providing additional anti-inflammatory and anti-aging properties.

Ingredients:

1 cup mango (frozen or fresh with peel and pit removed) (beta-carotene)
1 teaspoon fresh ginger (peeled and grated)
1 small carrot (peeled and chopped) (beta-carotene)
1 Tablespoon chia seeds
1 cup water
¼ teaspoon turmeric (optional – yet highly recommended – it's delicious and full of anti-inflammatory properties)

Directions:

Put everything in a blender. Blend and pour.

Nutrient Facts:
230 calories
45 grams of carbohydrates
5 grams of fat
4 grams of protein
11 grams of fiber

Whether you're in the mood for a quick and sweet breakfast or a special dessert to finish off a light meal, allow this nutrient-dense smoothie to do the job.

Ingredients:

¾ cup canned pumpkin puree (beta-carotene)
1 Tablespoon ground flax seed
2 teaspoons honey
½ medium, ripe banana
1 teaspoon vanilla
1 teaspoon pumpkin pie spice
½ cup unsweetened almond milk

Directions:
Put everything in a blender. Blend and pour.

Nutrient Facts:
246 calories
45 grams of carbohydrates
6 grams of fat
9 grams of protein
11 grams of fiber

This summer smoothie has a mellow melon and banana flavor; and the squash and chia seeds provide a nice textural component.

Ingredients:

½ cup cantaloupe (rind and seeds removed, cut into cubes) (beta-carotene)
½ medium, ripe banana
½ orange (peel and seeds removed)
½ cup raw yellow squash (ends removed, cubed)
1 Tablespoon chia seeds
½ cup unsweetened almond milk or regular milk (dairy option) or water

Directions:

Put everything in a blender. Blend and pour.

Nutrient Facts:
236 calories
38 grams of carbohydrates
7 grams of fat
9 grams of protein
12 grams of fiber

15 Green Beta-Carotene Machine Smoothie

Thinking about beta-carotene often brings up images of orangey-yellow foods, so it may come as a surprise that this beta-carotene rich smoothie is all green. The green foods do wonders to protect our cells from damage.

Ingredients:

½ cup kale (only take the leaf part and leave out the stem) (beta-carotene)
½ cup tightly packed spinach (beta-carotene)
2 Tablespoons avocado (peel and pit removed)
½ medium, ripe banana
1 kiwi, skin removed
½ green apple (cored and cubed)
1 cup coconut water or regular water

Directions:

Put everything in a blender. Blend and pour.

Nutrient Facts:
157 calories
32 grams of carbohydrates
4 grams of fat
4 grams of protein
7 grams of fiber

TIP: Make multiple servings of your smoothie in your blender. For example, make two servings of the smoothie and put one serving in a mason jar or mug to bring to work or school. Now you have a meal or hearty snack on-the-go.

OMEGA-3

Omega-3: As we age, our skin loses moisture and elasticity which results in more wrinkles. **Omega-3 fatty acids** have been found to provide the skin with more moisture by keeping the cells of the epidermis (our top layer of skin) plump and hydrated. In addition, the fatty acids help keep the cell membrane strong which can act as a barrier to outside pathogens that may be harmful. Omega-3s also have anti-inflammatory compounds which can affect how healthy our skin looks and feels.

**The recommended daily allowance of alpha-linolenic acid, ALA, a part of the Omega-3 fatty acids is 1.6 grams daily for men and 1.1 grams daily for women, according to the US Food and Drug Administration.

Sources of ALA include:

Food	Grams (g) Per Serving	Percent Daily Value (Based off Male)
Walnuts, 1 ounce	2.5	156
Chia Seeds, 1 ounce	4.5	281
Ground Flaxseeds, 2 Tablespoons	1.6	100

While oils and nuts are good sources of ALAs, consuming them in moderation is still important due to their high caloric value.

An easy way to keep skin looking hydrated and glowing is to add omega-3 rich chia seeds to your diet.

Ingredients:

½ cup mango (frozen or fresh with peel and pit removed)
1 cup pineapple (canned and drained or fresh with peel removed and cubed)
1 Tablespoon chia seeds (Omega-3)
1 cup coconut water or regular water

Directions:
Put everything in a blender. Blend and pour.

Nutrient Facts:
200 calories
41 grams of carbohydrates
5 grams of fat
4 grams of protein
9 grams of fiber

These ingredients make a perfect on-the-go snack for energy, and by blending them together into a smoothie, they become a perfect "on the go" snack for convenience. The omega-3 rich walnuts plus the super easy prep make this a stress-free and "wrinkle-free" recipe.

Ingredients:

4 halves walnuts (omega-3)
1 cup fresh or frozen blackberries
½ medium, ripe banana
½ cup unsweetened almond milk or regular milk (dairy option)

Directions:
Put everything in a blender. Blend and pour.

Nutrient Facts:
236 calories
31 grams of carbohydrates
11 grams of fat
9 grams of protein
12 grams of fiber

18 Strawberry, Basil, and Chia Smoothie

This is a refined twist on the classic strawberry smoothie. Adding fresh herbs to smoothies provide a bit of tasteful elegance. The frozen fruit gives an extra slushy texture.

Nutrient Facts:
151 calories
23 grams of carbohydrates
6 grams of fat
4 grams of protein
10 grams of fiber

Ingredients:

1 ½ cup frozen strawberries
4 leaves of basil
1 teaspoon lemon juice
1 Tablespoon chia seeds (omega-3)
¼ cup light coconut milk

Directions:
Put everything in a blender. Blend and pour.

19 Peanut Butter and Banana... and Squash Smoothie

Elvis would have approved of this smoothie because bananas and peanut butter were some of his favorite foods. The flavor of the squash fades away in the presence of the peanut butter, banana, and honey, and you can still feel good about getting in your veggies.

Ingredients:

1 small, ripe banana (6 inches)
½ cup raw yellow squash (ends removed, cubed)
1 Tablespoon peanut butter
1 Tablespoon ground flaxseed (omega-3)
½ cup unsweetened almond milk or regular milk (dairy option)
1 teaspoon honey

Directions:

Put everything in a blender. Blend and pour.

Nutrient Facts:
287 calories
35 grams of carbohydrates
14 grams of fat
11 grams of protein
8 grams of fiber

This is a delectable sweet treat with no added sugar. The dates are natures' sugary fruit-perfect for a sweet-tooth craving.

Ingredients:

5 dates (pitted)
4 halves walnuts (omega-3)
1 Tablespoon cacao powder
¼ teaspoon vanilla
½ cup unsweetened almond milk
Pinch of cinnamon

Directions:

Put everything in a blender. Blend and pour.

Nutrient Facts:
232 calories
38 grams of carbohydrates
8 grams of fat
8 grams of protein
7 grams of fiber

TIP: Some additional ideas for various heart-healthy fats to add to a smoothie.

Heart-Healthy Fats:
Chia seeds, Ground Flaxmeal, Hemp Seeds, Sunflower Seeds, Peanut Butter, Almond Butter, other Nut Butters, Walnuts, Almonds, Pecans, Avocado, Olive Oil, Coconut Oil

POLYPHENOLS

Polyphenols are antioxidants that protect the body from oxidizing agents; and can protect the skin and cells from tissue damage. Polyphenols also block the enzymes and deactivate substances that promote certain cancerous growths. With that said, the antioxidants have the perfect properties for keeping our skin lustrous and radiant.

***Polyphenols do not have a recommended daily value according to the US Food and Drug Administration. Regardless, the following foods and drinks contain good amounts of polyphenols.

FOOD

Blackberries	Dates	Kale
Blueberries	Cacao	Spinach
Pomegranates	Tea	Red Cabbage
Strawberries	Coffee	Basil
Tart Cherries		

Isn't it great that cacao protects the skin and cells, and makes everything taste ten times better?

Ingredients:

1 medium, ripe banana
6 fresh or frozen strawberries (polyphenols)
1 Tablespoon cacao powder (polyphenols)
½ Tablespoon chia seeds
1 cup unsweetened almond milk or regular milk (dairy option)

Directions:
Put everything in a blender. Blend and pour.

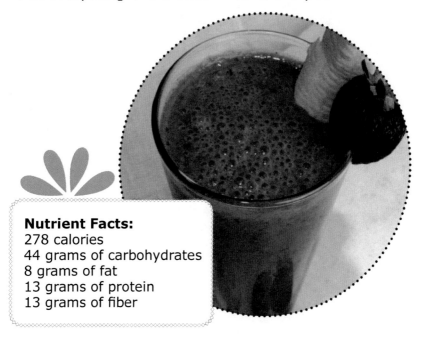

Nutrient Facts:
278 calories
44 grams of carbohydrates
8 grams of fat
13 grams of protein
13 grams of fiber

Coffee Date Smoothie

Impress your next coffee date with this Coffee Date Smoothie. The notes of coconut add an exceptional touch of flavor.

Ingredients:

3 dates (pitted) (polyphenols)
½ medium, ripe banana
1 Tablespoon unsweetened coconut flakes
1 Tablespoon cacao powder (polyphenols)
½ cup coconut yogurt or Greek style yogurt (dairy option)
¼ cup coffee (brewed and chilled) (polyphenols)
½ cup coconut milk or regular milk (dairy option)
1 teaspoon of cacao nibs (optional)

Directions:

Put everything except cacao nibs in a blender. Blend and pour. Sprinkle cacao nibs over the top.

Nutrient Facts:
283 calories
45 grams of carbohydrates
4 grams of fat
17 grams of protein
6 grams of fiber

23 Tart Cherry and Cacao Bliss Smoothie

Cherries and cacao go hand in hand flavor wise. And they are both packed with polyphenols to maintain brilliant skin. Chocolate covered cherries just make so much sense for gorgeous skin health. Here's a drink version of that sweet delight.

Ingredients:

1 cup frozen tart cherries (pitted) (polyphenols)
½ medium, ripe banana
1 Tablespoon chia seeds
1 Tablespoon cacao powder (polyphenols)
½ cup water

Directions:
Put everything in a blender. Blend and pour.

Nutrient Facts:
217 calories
40 grams of carbohydrates
6 grams of fat
5 grams of protein
11 grams of fiber

Green Tea, Blueberry, and Banana Shebang Smoothie

Any type of green tea will work perfectly in this smoothie. For additional richness and creaminess, try using matcha green tea powder, found in some specialty stores.

Ingredients:

½ cup green tea (brewed and chilled) (polyphenols)
½ cup coconut yogurt or Greek style yogurt (dairy option)
½ cup fresh or frozen blueberries (polyphenols)
1 medium, ripe banana
1 Tablespoon ground flax seed

Directions:
Put everything in a blender. Blend and pour.

Nutrient Facts:
250 calories
44 grams of carbohydrates
4 grams of fat
4 grams of protein
7 grams of fiber

Pomegranate and blackberries have a "black belt" in protecting skin and cells from oxidative stress.

Ingredients:

½ cup fresh or frozen blackberries (polyphenols)
½ fresh or ½ cup frozen pomegranate seeds (seeds removed from husk if using fresh) (polyphenols)
½ cucumber (peeled)
1 Tablespoon chia seeds
½ cup water

Directions:
Put everything in a blender. Blend and pour.

Nutrient Facts:
232 calories
42 grams of carbohydrates
7 grams of fat
7 grams of protein
16 grams of fiber

CONCLUSION:

———————⚬✍⚬———————

Now you know what foods and nutrients will bring extra life, elasticity, and vivacity to your skin for an age-defying glow. Make sure to incorporate at least one or more of these foods into your daily diet to keep your skin lively and fresh. The more fruits, vegetables, nuts and seeds that you eat on a daily basis - the more your skin and health will benefit from all of the antioxidants, phytochemicals, vitamins, and minerals in those foods. Your body will be an absorbing machine of health and wellness. Drink up to your youth, and enjoy your "Smoothie Journey"!

BIOGRAPHY:

Sarah Koszyk, MA, RDN, is an award-winning registered dietitian/nutritionist specializing in weight management and sports nutrition. Sarah is founder of **Family. Food. Fiesta.** providing families with delicious and healthy recipes, meal plans, and kid cooking videos in order to optimize one's performance and nutrition. Sarah coaches athletes, adults, and pediatrics towards their health and wellness goals. With a passion for delicious food that nourishes the body, mind, and soul-Sarah emphasizes a holistic approach to learn a sustainable, lifelong, positive relationship with food as fuel for the body. She has been featured on Bay Sunday CBS San Francisco, Al Despertar Univision 41, in Runner's World, Today's Dietitian, and more. She has a monthly column in UltraRunning Magazine, NutritionJobs, and ExerciseJobs. She co-wrote **Brain Food: 10 Simple Foods That Will Increase Your Focus, Improve Your Memory And Decrease Depression.** Sarah contributed to **Whole Body Reboot: The Peruvian Superfoods Diet To Detoxify, Energize, And Supercharge Fat Loss.**

Connect with her at **www.SarahKoszyk.com** and join her fiesta.

ACKNOWLEDGEMENTS:

I would like to sincerely thank Leah Walton, who interned with me. She assisted with some of the smoothie recipes and photos. Leah is now a Registered Dietitian living in San Francisco, CA. She completed her Bachelor of Science and Dietetic Internship at San Francisco State University (SFSU). Her passions include lifestyle development, yoga, soccer, live music, traveling, cooking and sharing new recipes with friends and clients. Leah is a supporter of food justice efforts and believes everyone has the right to healthy and wholesome nutrition. I would like to thank all the amazing interns at SFSU for making such a huge impact in the dietetic field.

I would also like to thank my mom, Carol Koszyk, for her precise editing of this book and her diligent attention to detail. Without her, I wouldn't be where I am today.

Manufactured by Amazon.ca
Bolton, ON

20582845R00036